This Ancestry Tracker Belongs To:

If you want to understand today,
you have to search yesterday.

-Pearl S. Buck

My Family

My Family

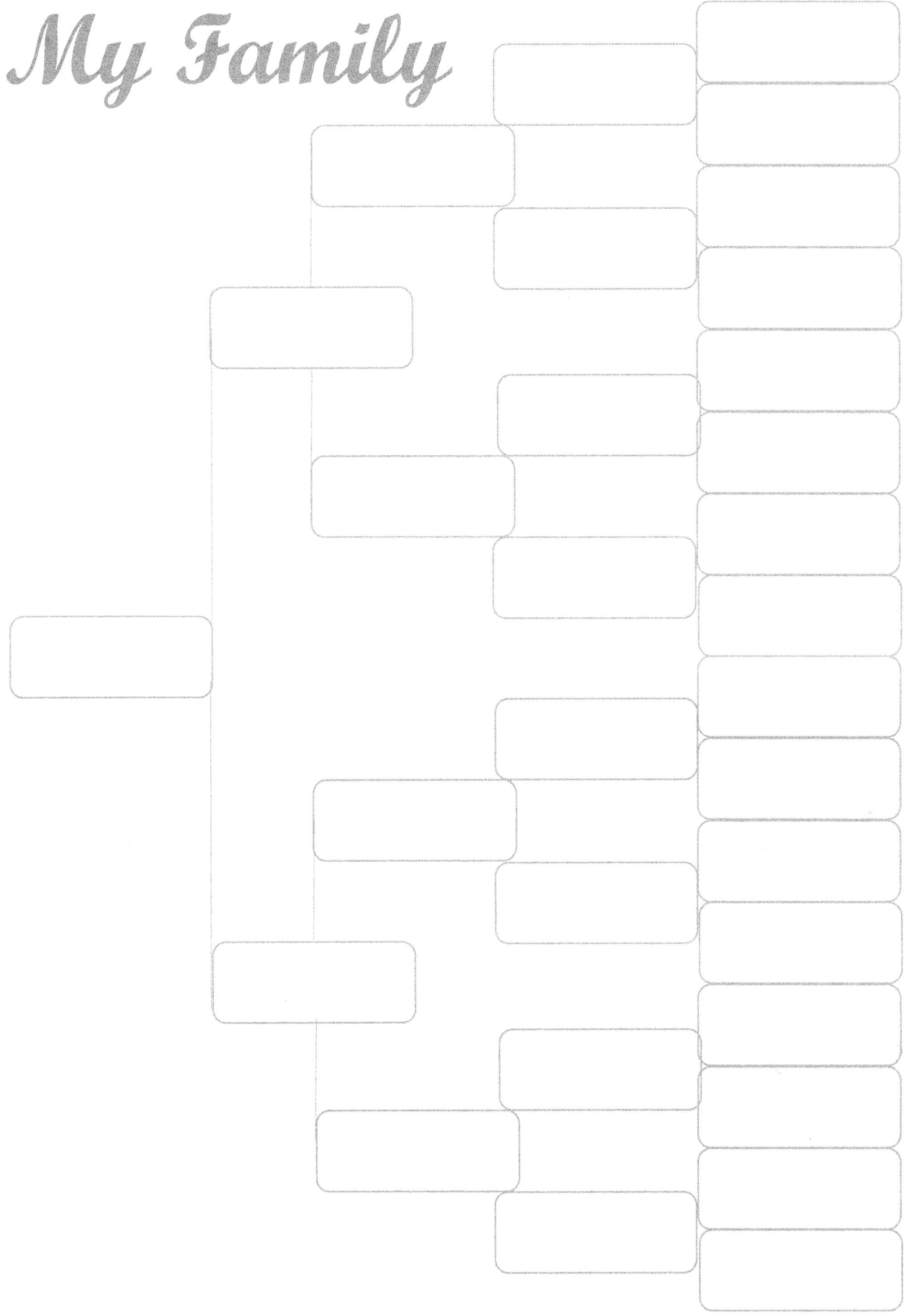

My Story

My Story

Date   Timeline of Life Events

Date   Timeline of Life Events

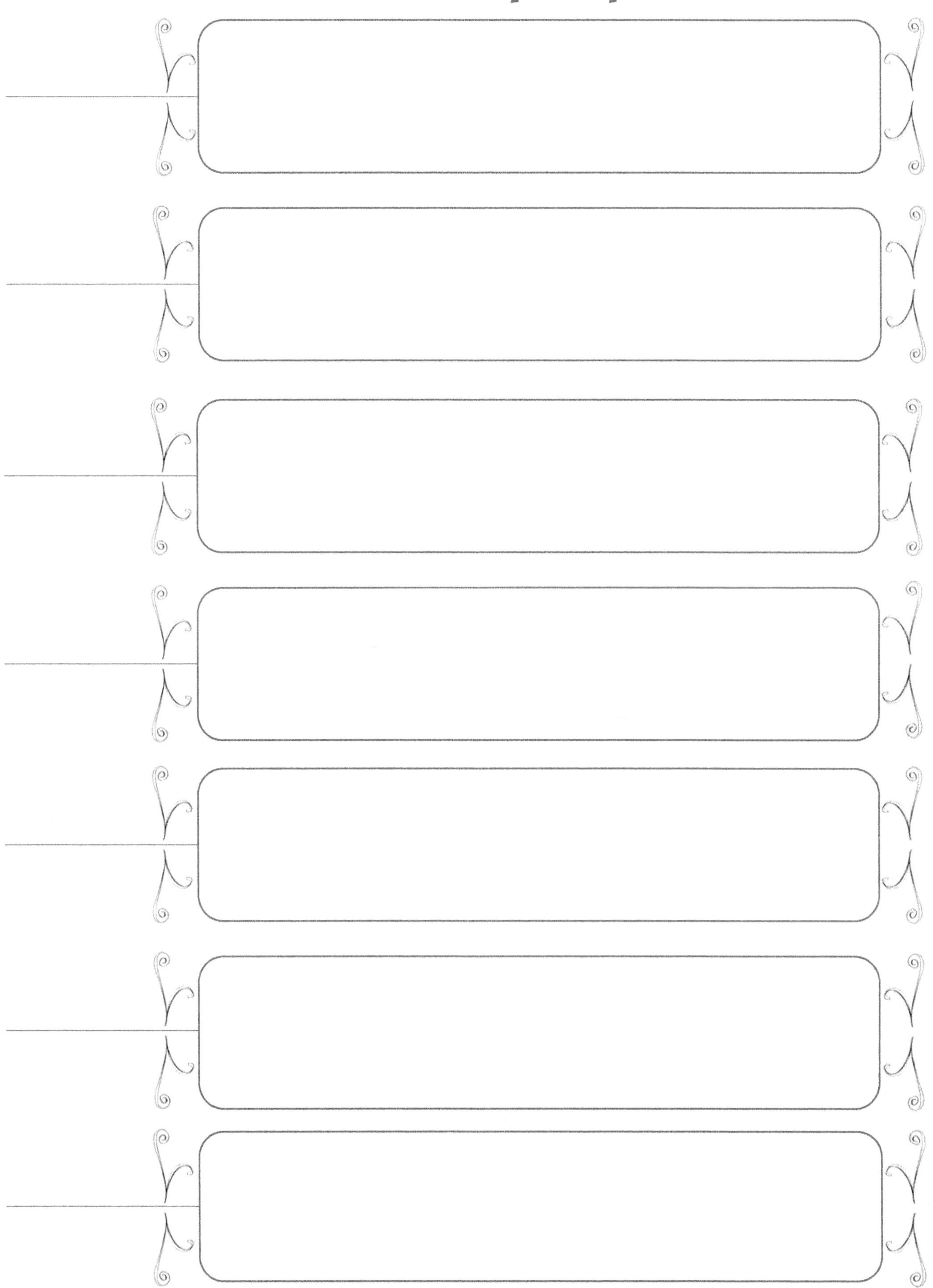

Date   Timeline of Life Events

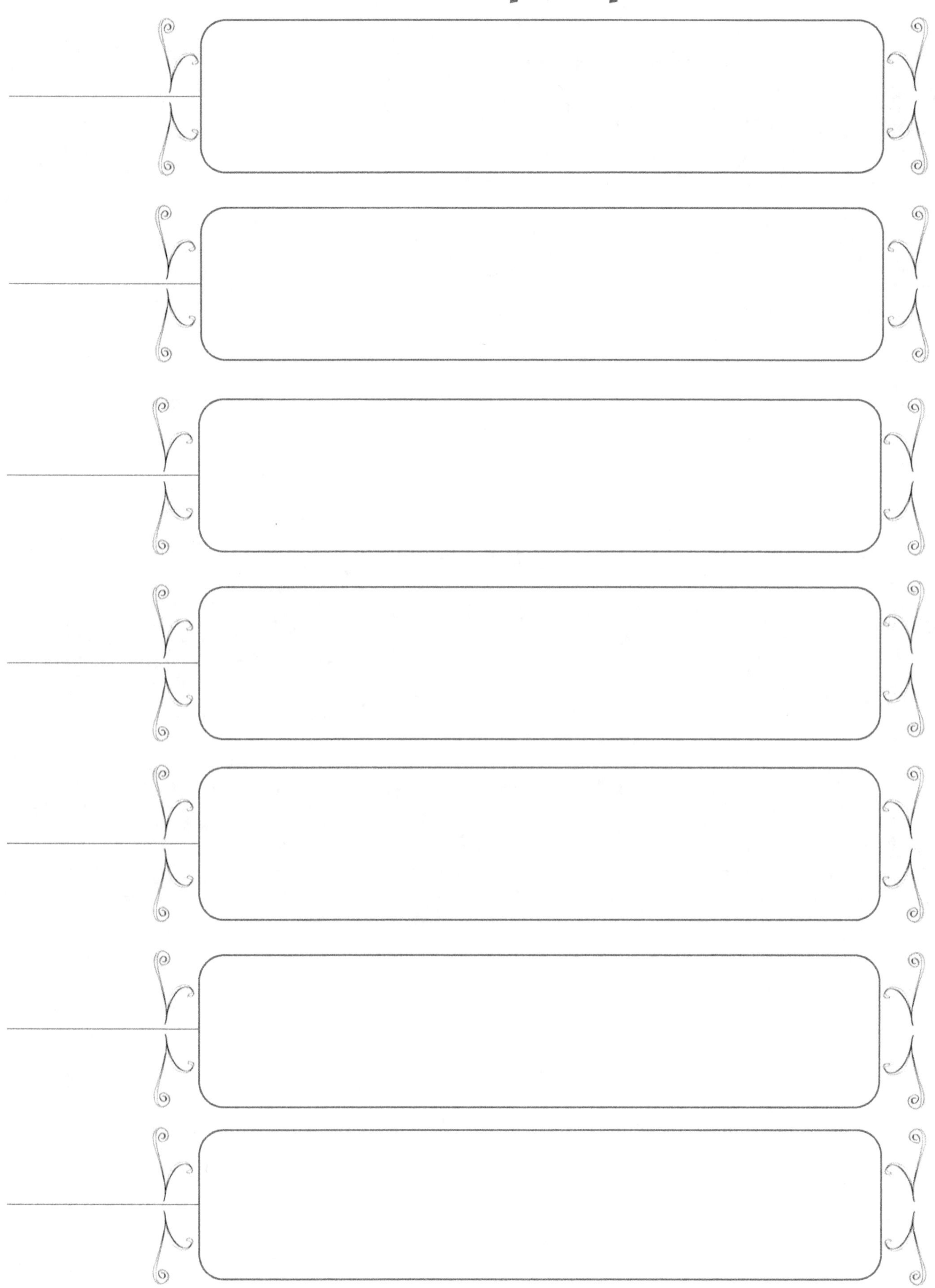

Date   Timeline of Life Events

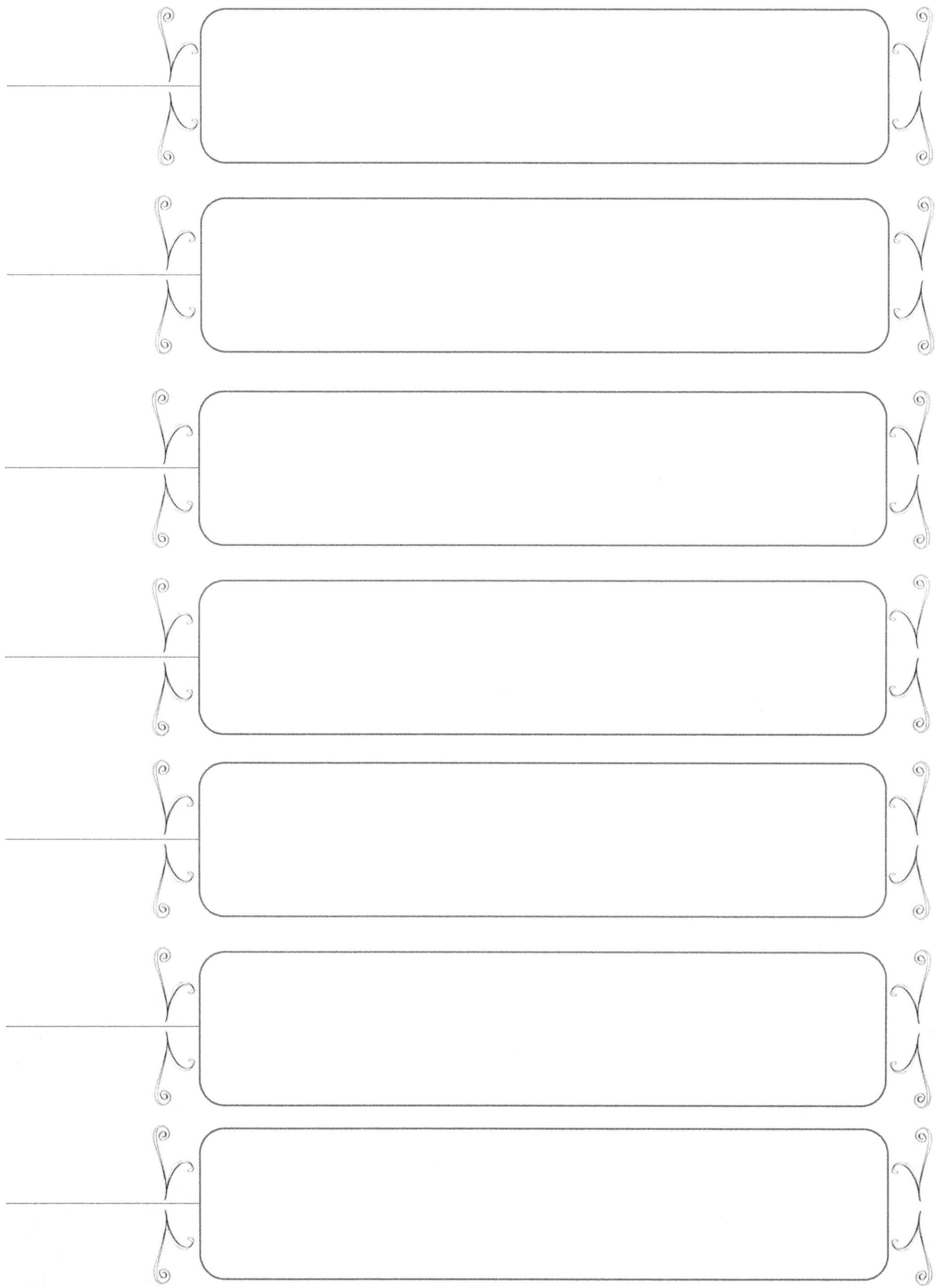

Date   Timeline of Life Events

Date   Timeline of Life Events

Ancestor's Full Name: _______________

Relationship: _______________ ☐ Paternal ☐ Maternal

Date of Birth: Birthplace: Date of Death:

Parents

Marriages

Date: Spouse:

Date: Spouse:

Date: Spouse:

Date: Spouse:

Siblings

Name	DOB
Name	DOB
Name	DOB
Name	DOB
Name	DOB
Name	DOB
Name	DOB
Name	DOB

Children

Name	DOB
Name	DOB
Name	DOB
Name	DOB
Name	DOB
Name	DOB
Name	DOB

Notes

Source of Information

	Birth Certificate		Ancestry DNA
	Death Certificate		Newspaper Article
	Marriage Certificate		23 & Me
	Obituary		Deeds/Land Records
	Grave Marker		Military Records
	Census		Google/Internet
	Will/Probate Records		Other

Leads

Source of Information

	Birth Certificate		Ancestry DNA
	Death Certificate		Newspaper Article
	Marriage Certificate		23 & Me
	Obituary		Deeds/Land Records
	Grave Marker		Military Records
	Census		Google/Internet
	Will/Probate Records		Other

Leads

Photos/Documents

Description

Photos/Documents

Description

Ancestor's Full Name: ____________________

Relationship: ____________ ☐ Paternal ☐ Maternal

Date of Birth: Birthplace: Date of Death:

Parents

Marriages

Date: Spouse:

Date: Spouse:

Date: Spouse:

Date: Spouse:

Siblings

Name	DOB
Name	DOB
Name	DOB
Name	DOB
Name	DOB
Name	DOB
Name	DOB
Name	DOB

Children

Name	DOB
Name	DOB
Name	DOB
Name	DOB
Name	DOB
Name	DOB
Name	DOB

Notes

Source of Information

	Birth Certificate		Ancestry DNA
	Death Certificate		Newspaper Article
	Marriage Certificate		23 & Me
	Obituary		Deeds/Land Records
	Grave Marker		Military Records
	Census		Google/Internet
	Will/Probate Records		Other

Leads

Source of Information

Birth Certificate	Ancestry DNA
Death Certificate	Newspaper Article
Marriage Certificate	23 & Me
Obituary	Deeds/Land Records
Grave Marker	Military Records
Census	Google/Internet
Will/Probate Records	Other

Leads

Photos/Documents

Description

Photos/Documents

Description

Ancestor's Full Name: _______________

Relationship: _______________ ☐ Paternal ☐ Maternal

Date of Birth: Birthplace: Date of Death:

Parents

Marriages

Date: Spouse:

Date: Spouse:

Date: Spouse:

Date: Spouse:

Siblings

Name	DOB
Name	DOB
Name	DOB
Name	DOB
Name	DOB
Name	DOB
Name	DOB

Children

Name	DOB
Name	DOB
Name	DOB
Name	DOB
Name	DOB
Name	DOB
Name	DOB

Notes

Source of Information

	Birth Certificate			Ancestry DNA
	Death Certificate			Newspaper Article
	Marriage Certificate			23 & Me
	Obituary			Deeds/Land Records
	Grave Marker			Military Records
	Census			Google/Internet
	Will/Probate Records			Other

Leads

Source of Information

	Birth Certificate
	Death Certificate
	Marriage Certificate
	Obituary
	Grave Marker
	Census
	Will/Probate Records

	Ancestry DNA
	Newspaper Article
	23 & Me
	Deeds/Land Records
	Military Records
	Google/Internet
	Other

Leads

Photos / Documents

Description

Photos/Documents

Description

Ancestor's Full Name: _______________

Relationship: _______________ ☐ Paternal ☐ Maternal

Date of Birth: ___________ Birthplace: ___________ Date of Death: ___________

Parents

| |
| |
| |
| |

Marriages

Date: ___________ Spouse: ___________

Date: ___________ Spouse: ___________

Date: ___________ Spouse: ___________

Date: ___________ Spouse: ___________

Siblings

Name	DOB
Name	DOB
Name	DOB
Name	DOB
Name	DOB
Name	DOB
Name	DOB
Name	DOB

Children

Name	DOB
Name	DOB
Name	DOB
Name	DOB
Name	DOB
Name	DOB
Name	DOB
Name	DOB

Notes

	Birth Certificate		Ancestry DNA
	Death Certificate		Newspaper Article
	Marriage Certificate		23 & Me
	Obituary		Deeds/Land Records
	Grave Marker		Military Records
	Census		Google/Internet
	Will/Probate Records		Other

Leads

Source of Information

	Birth Certificate		Ancestry DNA
	Death Certificate		Newspaper Article
	Marriage Certificate		23 & Me
	Obituary		Deeds/Land Records
	Grave Marker		Military Records
	Census		Google/Internet
	Will/Probate Records		Other

Leads

Photos/Documents

Description

Photos / Documents

Description

Ancestor's Full Name: _______________

Relationship: _______________ ☐ Paternal ☐ Maternal

Date of Birth: Birthplace: Date of Death:

Parents

Marriages

Date: Spouse:

Date: Spouse:

Date: Spouse:

Date: Spouse:

Siblings

Name   DOB

Name   DOB

Name   DOB

Name   DOB

Name   DOB

Name   DOB

Name   DOB

Name   DOB

Children

Name   DOB

Name   DOB

Name   DOB

Name   DOB

Name   DOB

Name   DOB

Name   DOB

Name   DOB

Notes

Source of Information

	Birth Certificate			Ancestry DNA
	Death Certificate			Newspaper Article
	Marriage Certificate			23 & Me
	Obituary			Deeds/Land Records
	Grave Marker			Military Records
	Census			Google/Internet
	Will/Probate Records			Other

Leads

Source of Information

	Birth Certificate			Ancestry DNA
	Death Certificate			Newspaper Article
	Marriage Certificate			23 & Me
	Obituary			Deeds/Land Records
	Grave Marker			Military Records
	Census			Google/Internet
	Will/Probate Records			Other

Leads

Photos/Documents

Description

Photos/Documents

Description

Ancestor's Full Name: ___________________

Relationship: ___________________ ☐ Paternal ☐ Maternal

Date of Birth: ___________ Birthplace: ___________ Date of Death: ___________

Parents

Marriages

Date: ___________ Spouse: ___________

Date: ___________ Spouse: ___________

Date: ___________ Spouse: ___________

Date: ___________ Spouse: ___________

Siblings

Name	DOB
Name	DOB
Name	DOB
Name	DOB
Name	DOB
Name	DOB
Name	DOB
Name	DOB

Children

Name	DOB
Name	DOB
Name	DOB
Name	DOB
Name	DOB
Name	DOB
Name	DOB
Name	DOB

Notes

family
BLESSINGS

Source of Information

	Birth Certificate		Ancestry DNA
	Death Certificate		Newspaper Article
	Marriage Certificate		23 & Me
	Obituary		Deeds/Land Records
	Grave Marker		Military Records
	Census		Google/Internet
	Will/Probate Records		Other

Leads

Source of Information

	Birth Certificate		Ancestry DNA
	Death Certificate		Newspaper Article
	Marriage Certificate		23 & Me
	Obituary		Deeds/Land Records
	Grave Marker		Military Records
	Census		Google/Internet
	Will/Probate Records		Other

Leads

Photos/Documents

Description

Photos/Documents

Description

Ancestor's Full Name:

Relationship: ☐ Paternal ☐ Maternal

Date of Birth: Birthplace: Date of Death:

Parents

Marriages

Date: Spouse:

Date: Spouse:

Date: Spouse:

Date: Spouse:

Siblings

Name	DOB
Name	DOB
Name	DOB
Name	DOB
Name	DOB
Name	DOB
Name	DOB

Children

Name	DOB
Name	DOB
Name	DOB
Name	DOB
Name	DOB
Name	DOB
Name	DOB

Notes

Source of Information

	Birth Certificate		Ancestry DNA
	Death Certificate		Newspaper Article
	Marriage Certificate		23 & Me
	Obituary		Deeds/Land Records
	Grave Marker		Military Records
	Census		Google/Internet
	Will/Probate Records		Other

Leads

Source of Information

	Birth Certificate			Ancestry DNA
	Death Certificate			Newspaper Article
	Marriage Certificate			23 & Me
	Obituary			Deeds/Land Records
	Grave Marker			Military Records
	Census			Google/Internet
	Will/Probate Records			Other

Leads

Photos/Documents

Description

Photos/Documents

Description

Ancestor's Full Name: ___________

Relationship: ___________ ☐ Paternal ☐ Maternal

Date of Birth: Birthplace: Date of Death:

Parents

Marriages

Date: Spouse:

Date: Spouse:

Date: Spouse:

Date: Spouse:

Siblings

Name	DOB
Name	DOB
Name	DOB
Name	DOB
Name	DOB
Name	DOB
Name	DOB
Name	DOB

Children

Name	DOB
Name	DOB
Name	DOB
Name	DOB
Name	DOB
Name	DOB
Name	DOB
Name	DOB

Notes

Source of Information

	Birth Certificate		Ancestry DNA
	Death Certificate		Newspaper Article
	Marriage Certificate		23 & Me
	Obituary		Deeds/Land Records
	Grave Marker		Military Records
	Census		Google/Internet
	Will/Probate Records		Other

Leads

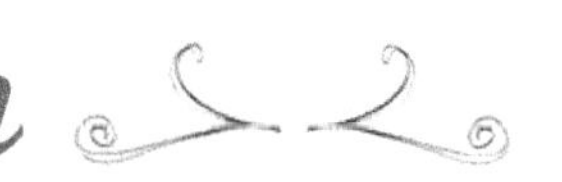

Source of Information

	Birth Certificate		Ancestry DNA
	Death Certificate		Newspaper Article
	Marriage Certificate		23 & Me
	Obituary		Deeds/Land Records
	Grave Marker		Military Records
	Census		Google/Internet
	Will/Probate Records		Other

Leads

Photos/Documents

Description

Photos/Documents

Description

Ancestor's Full Name: _______________

Relationship: _______________ ☐ Paternal ☐ Maternal

Date of Birth: _______________ Birthplace: _______________ Date of Death: _______________

Parents

Marriages

Date: Spouse:

Date: Spouse:

Date: Spouse:

Date: Spouse:

Siblings

Name	DOB
Name	DOB
Name	DOB
Name	DOB
Name	DOB
Name	DOB
Name	DOB
Name	DOB

Children

Name	DOB
Name	DOB
Name	DOB
Name	DOB
Name	DOB
Name	DOB
Name	DOB
Name	DOB

Notes

Source of Information

	Birth Certificate		Ancestry DNA
	Death Certificate		Newspaper Article
	Marriage Certificate		23 & Me
	Obituary		Deeds/Land Records
	Grave Marker		Military Records
	Census		Google/Internet
	Will/Probate Records		Other

Leads

Source of Information

	Birth Certificate
	Death Certificate
	Marriage Certificate
	Obituary
	Grave Marker
	Census
	Will/Probate Records

	Ancestry DNA
	Newspaper Article
	23 & Me
	Deeds/Land Records
	Military Records
	Google/Internet
	Other

Leads

Photos/Documents

Description

Photos/Documents

Description

Ancestor's Full Name: ______________________

Relationship: ______________ ☐ Paternal ☐ Maternal

Date of Birth: _______ Birthplace: _______ Date of Death: _______

Parents

| |
| |
| |
| |

Marriages

Date:	Spouse:
Date:	Spouse:
Date:	Spouse:
Date:	Spouse:

Siblings

Name	DOB
Name	DOB
Name	DOB
Name	DOB
Name	DOB
Name	DOB
Name	DOB
Name	DOB

Children

Name	DOB
Name	DOB
Name	DOB
Name	DOB
Name	DOB
Name	DOB
Name	DOB
Name	DOB

Notes

Source of Information

	Birth Certificate		Ancestry DNA
	Death Certificate		Newspaper Article
	Marriage Certificate		23 & Me
	Obituary		Deeds/Land Records
	Grave Marker		Military Records
	Census		Google/Internet
	Will/Probate Records		Other

Leads

Source of Information

	Birth Certificate		Ancestry DNA
	Death Certificate		Newspaper Article
	Marriage Certificate		23 & Me
	Obituary		Deeds/Land Records
	Grave Marker		Military Records
	Census		Google/Internet
	Will/Probate Records		Other

Leads

Photos/Documents

Description

Ancestor's Full Name:

Relationship: ________________ ☐ Paternal ☐ Maternal

Date of Birth: Birthplace: Date of Death:

Parents

Marriages

Date: Spouse:

Date: Spouse:

Date: Spouse:

Date: Spouse:

Siblings

Name	DOB
Name	DOB
Name	DOB
Name	DOB
Name	DOB
Name	DOB
Name	DOB

Children

Name	DOB
Name	DOB
Name	DOB
Name	DOB
Name	DOB
Name	DOB
Name	DOB

Notes

Source of Information

Birth Certificate	Ancestry DNA
Death Certificate	Newspaper Article
Marriage Certificate	23 & Me
Obituary	Deeds/Land Records
Grave Marker	Military Records
Census	Google/Internet
Will/Probate Records	Other

Leads

Source of Information

	Birth Certificate			Ancestry DNA
	Death Certificate			Newspaper Article
	Marriage Certificate			23 & Me
	Obituary			Deeds/Land Records
	Grave Marker			Military Records
	Census			Google/Internet
	Will/Probate Records			Other

Leads

Photos/Documents

Description

Photos/Documents

Description

Ancestor's Full Name: _______________

Relationship: _______________ ☐ Paternal ☐ Maternal

Date of Birth: Birthplace: Date of Death:

Parents

Marriages

Date: Spouse:

Date: Spouse:

Date: Spouse:

Date: Spouse:

Siblings

Name	DOB
Name	DOB
Name	DOB
Name	DOB
Name	DOB
Name	DOB
Name	DOB
Name	DOB

Children

Name	DOB
Name	DOB
Name	DOB
Name	DOB
Name	DOB
Name	DOB
Name	DOB
Name	DOB

Notes

Source of Information

	Birth Certificate	
	Death Certificate	
	Marriage Certificate	
	Obituary	
	Grave Marker	
	Census	
	Will/Probate Records	

	Ancestry DNA	
	Newspaper Article	
	23 & Me	
	Deeds/Land Records	
	Military Records	
	Google/Internet	
	Other	

Leads

Source of Information

	Birth Certificate
	Death Certificate
	Marriage Certificate
	Obituary
	Grave Marker
	Census
	Will/Probate Records

	Ancestry DNA
	Newspaper Article
	23 & Me
	Deeds/Land Records
	Military Records
	Google/Internet
	Other

Leads

Photos/Documents

Description

Photos/Documents

Description

Ancestor's Full Name:

Relationship: ______________________ ☐ Paternal ☐ Maternal

Date of Birth: Birthplace: Date of Death:

Parents

Marriages

Date: Spouse:

Date: Spouse:

Date: Spouse:

Date: Spouse:

Siblings

Name	DOB
Name	DOB
Name	DOB
Name	DOB
Name	DOB
Name	DOB
Name	DOB
Name	DOB

Children

Name	DOB
Name	DOB
Name	DOB
Name	DOB
Name	DOB
Name	DOB
Name	DOB
Name	DOB

Notes

Source of Information

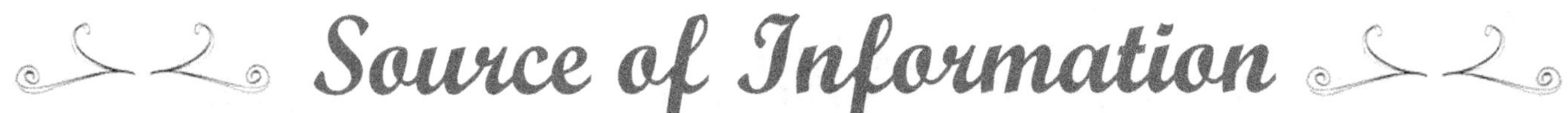

	Birth Certificate		Ancestry DNA
	Death Certificate		Newspaper Article
	Marriage Certificate		23 & Me
	Obituary		Deeds/Land Records
	Grave Marker		Military Records
	Census		Google/Internet
	Will/Probate Records		Other

Leads

Source of Information

	Birth Certificate			Ancestry DNA
	Death Certificate			Newspaper Article
	Marriage Certificate			23 & Me
	Obituary			Deeds/Land Records
	Grave Marker			Military Records
	Census			Google/Internet
	Will/Probate Records			Other

Leads

Photos/Documents

Description

Photos/Documents

Description

Notes